THE RELEVANT CHURCH

THE CHURCH OF CHRIST BEYOND CRISIS

Owusu Amoateng Kofi

PAL PUBLICATION

Contents

Foreword

"The Relevant Church," authored by Owusu Amoateng Kofi, is a reflection of the Church's response to the Covid-19 pandemic and beyond.

He invites the church for a serious reflection in asking the following questions:

-       What should the Church be like after covid-19?

-       How should the Church, after Covid-19, operate?

-       What can the Church, after Covid-19, do to maintain relevance?

-       What can the Church, after Covid-19, do to attract others?

In the whole book, the author seeks to answer the issues he has raised in the foregoing questions:

In chapter 1 – "A Call to Advance Beyond Crisis." The author invites believers to accept two challenges:" First, that God is going to advance His kingdom through us (Matt. 16:19; Luke 20:19; 2 Cor. 5:20)." This calls for a deeper work of the Holy Spirit in the life of every believer. Secondly, that believers' advancement should be in alignment with God's Kingdom.

In chapter 2 – "Relevance Matters." The relevant church should see itself as the true "salt of the earth and light of the world" (Matt. 5:13-16).

Chapter 3 – "Understanding the Times and the Seasons." Our understanding of the times and the seasons mean our serious study of how to relate to people in a much more sensitive way to enable them to understand their need for our Savior as their only hope in life. Remember how Jesus dialogued with the woman at Jacob's Well in John until she saw who Jesus was and eventually yielded her life to Him.

Chapter 4 – "Maintaining Spiritual Relevance." "You are relevant if you add flavor or taste to the earth," says the author. The author suggests the following ways to make the believer spiritually relevant:

a)   Prayer and the Holy Spirit – the author says, "Prayer is a Kingdom system that authorizes God's power on earth." "The more believers engage in prayer, worship and fasting, it increases the power of God on earth, as this is what brings awakening and revival."

a)   The Word of God – "The relevant church must know how to effectively use God's Word."

a.   Quote it in prayer.

b.   Use it in worship and in praises.

c.   Attack the evil one with the word – "It is written..." as Jesus did in Matt. 4:1-11.

d.   Use the Word in witnessing to the lost.

e.   Teach the Word in the church and In-House Groups.

In chapter 5 – "Maintaining the Physical Relevance." He suggests the following:

a)   The Church must do away with complacency. The complacency may include laziness, disunity, and all manner of excuses that have weakened the Church before the pandemic.

b)   Attitude – "The most significant change we need in these last days, in my opinion... We do not need to worry so much about the devil but our attitude. We must change our attitude about the things of God." The author contends.

a)   Time, talent and treasure – "God's responsibility is to give gifts, talents, and wisdom to His people, and our responsibility is to use these gifts, talents, and skills to solve problems in the world to advance His Kingdom on earth."

b)   The Church must pursue unity – "The Church beyond crisis must pursue oneness and unity." There must be oneness of purpose, oneness of passion and oneness of power. "The holy Spirit cannot work in a disunited Church." Mark 3:23-26; 1 Cor. 3:1-7. "The Church beyond crisis must preach Christ and practice genuine love."

Chapter 6 – "Maintaining Strategic Relevance." "God is not a secret to be kept. As a believer, you must make Him known." The author suggests the following to help maintain strategic relevance.

a)   Go to where the fishes (souls) are.

b)   The Church must be involved in the community to remain relevant. Provide the real needs of the community – food, clothes, and daily provision.

c)   Innovation and change – during the pandemic, churches were forced to find new ways to do ministry. It has taught the Church to be more innovative in doing ministry. "Technology alone insists that you change your approach to ministry" – Dan Reiland.

Chapter 7 – "Standard Bearers." "... I will define the majority of Christians by two standards. First, there are Christians who live by the standard of popular opinions and emotions... however, there is a third standard by which every believer and church must raise. This is the standard of God's Word and revelation of Christ."

The author suggests three essential standards the Church needs to lift in high esteem. They are Scripture, the Spirit, and Sacrifice and Commitment. He quotes Romans 12:1 to buttress his appeal.

Chapter 8 – "Leadership Change." The author emphasizes the fact that, "One of the biggest challenges of the Church becoming relevant or influential beyond crisis is leadership. The relevant church needs relevant leaders. He defines them as, "leaders who will understand, and most importantly, implement the mind of God." The author suggests seven key things for a leader to maintain relevance at such a time.

a)   What I teach – Teach the accurate Word of God, leading to the raising of mature Christians who fit the standard of the Holy Spirit. This is when the leader's fruit abides (John 15:16).

b)   How to live – "We need leaders who practice what they preach." We need leaders with integrity, character, self-control, and discipline today more than ever before."

c)   My purpose in life – "Leaders who have a purpose will help pull people up in the midst of the worldwide crisis."

d)   My faith – "We need faith-filled leaders, especially in times of crisis. This is because the central task of a leader is to imagine a better future beyond challenges and inspire their followers to get there."

e)   Patience – Doug Morgan said, "True leaders recognized that patience enables them to take stock of the situation, understand what is required, and wait while building the capacity to take appropriate, effective action. By demonstrating patience, leaders reinforce the importance of focusing on long-term outcomes."

f)   Love – "leadership has a powerful impact when the people feel loved."

g)   Endurance – Endurance grows when we reflect on the heroes of our historic faith, who persevered in their generation in spite of the challenges they encountered in their lives and ministries. Our greatest motivation in endurance is our Lord and Savior Jesus Christ. Let us fix our eyes on Him for inspiration as we go through all the challenges of life – Hebrews 12:2.

Chapter 9 – "A revival generation." The writer shares ten (10) key characteristics of a new revival generation God is raising.

We will also win; you were born and created in Christ to win in all situations, including the Covid-19 pandemic.

Serve the Lord with Apostolic ambition! SHALOM!

Rev. Dr. Steve Asante,

Past President, Ghana Baptist Convention

Past National Director, Ghana Evangelism committee

stevekasante49@yahoo.com

Introduction

THIS MANUSCRIPT IS ONE of my books born due to the Covid – 19 pandemic in December 2019. The fundamental truth is that things will not be the same again, whether we like it or not. The world as we know it has shifted, including everything in it.

A shift is a change in the atmosphere, and since the atmosphere determines everything, you must understand that Coronavirus has come to change our usual way of life.

For instance, a global shift means that the systems that run the world will not be the same ever again.

A market shift, for instance, means the workplace is not going to be the same again. We are moving into cashless systems in the marketplace, and people will be working more from home than the usual office styles that we have always known.

As a result, those working in the hospitality and airline industry must all shift to remain relevant.

As I write this book for the Church of Christ specifically, every believer needs to note that this shift or change in the atmosphere affects us. Therefore, a Kingdom shift means a need for the Church to shift to remain relevant in societies and communities.

Jesus indeed said in **Matthew 18:16**, "I will build my church, and the gates of hell shall not prevail against it." However, this does not mean the Church should walk in ignorance.

In the words of Thomas Jefferson, "In matters of style, swim with the current; in matters of principle, stand like a rock." This quote means the Church must shift with the current trends while remaining strong like a rock amid changing times like these.

This global crisis has stared my heart deeply to reflect on the state of the Church in asking these questions;

- **What should the Church be like after Covid-19?**

- **How should the Church after Covid-19 operate?**

- **What can the Church after Covid-19 do to maintain relevance?**

- **What can the Church after Covid-19 do to attract others?**

These and more are the bedrock of this book to enable you to shift to remain relevant wherever you are as a church or Christian.

I sincerely pray that this book will help you as a church leader, worker, and believer in Christ. May the Spirit of the Lord come fresh upon you.

One

A Call to Advance Beyond Crisis

• • • • ● ● • ● ● • • •

AMID THE WORLD IN crisis, God calls on you, the Church, to advance His Kingdom on earth. What we are seeing in the world today is the groaning of creation (frustrations), and creation is groaning for the manifestation of the children of God and the end times. **1 Peter 4:7, Romans 8:19-22**

For the creation waits in eager expectation for the children of God to be revealed. For the creation was subjected to frustration, not by its own choice, but by the will of the one who subjected it, in hope

[21] that the creation itself will be liberated from its bondage to decay and brought into the freedom and glory of the children of God. [22] We know that the whole creation has been groaning as in the pains of childbirth right up to the present time.

Since the fall of man (Adam), creation has never been able to realize its God-intended purpose and potential. Instead, it has been subjected to frustration, including the progressive corruption and deterioration of the natural world up until today(now).

Prophetically, God does not want us (Church) to see what is happening in the world as a negative cry of expectation but as a positive cry of eager anticipation.

Instead, what we are witnessing is likened to childbirth pains. Spiritually, birth pains represent two key things

1. It represents looking forward to the second coming of Christ, which will end evil in the world. **Mark 13:8**

2. Birth pains usually lead to birth, not death, so there is hope for revival and awakening in our cities and nations as the Church ceases this as an opportunity to advance God's Kingdom on earth.

Prophetically, there are two key things I see in the midst of this pandemic and especially beyond. Firstly, God will advance His Kingdom through us, and secondly, your advancement will be in alignment with His Kingdom.

There are two prophecies here; permit me to exploit them further.

First, God is going to advance His Kingdom through the Church.

Every believer needs to understand this truth, and that is, God has already permitted us to advance His Kingdom agenda on earth beyond crisis.

Matthew 16:19 says I will give you the keys of the Kingdom of heaven; and whatever you bind on earth shall have been bound in heaven, and whatever you loose on earth shall have been loosed in heaven."

Luke 10:19 says, Behold, I give you the authority to trample on serpents and scorpions, and over all the power of the enemy, and nothing shall by any means hurt you.

2 Corinthians 5:20, So we are now representatives of the Anointed One, the Liberating King; God has given us a charge to carry through our lives—urging all people on behalf of the Anointed to become reconciled to the Creator God.

As believers, we must be ready to carry God's end-time plan on earth through the indwelling Spirit of the Holy Ghost. However, this God's plan is not secured until the Spirt takes complete residence in us.

As we yield to Him and live in obedience to him rather than the flesh, then and only then shall we see God's kingdom manifestation in our cities and nations.

Therefore, the goal of every believer must include being led by the Spirit's power.

The prayer of every believer at such a time like this also needs to include that no matter what is happening in our lives, it should lead to the advancement of His Kingdom. So may even our sufferings lead to glory.

Paul puts it this way, "Now I want you to know, brothers and sisters,[] that what has happened to me has served to advance the gospel." **Philippians 1:12-18**

Secondly, your advancement will be in alignment with His Kingdom. As the Lord speaks to the Body of Christ in general, He also speaks to our individual needs. The Lord says I should tell somebody that there will be no more delay, reproach, or stagnancy as you align to His Kingdom.

Amid the storm, get ready to advance like the eagle. I see the believer move this year like the ways of the eagle in the air. The eagle is the only animal in the air that looks for storms to advance and progress.

> "But those who wait on the Lord
> Shall renew their strength; They
> shall mount up with wings like
> eagles, They shall run and not be
> weary, They shall walk and not
> faint." **Isaiah 40:31**

Therefore, I see a call for the Church to turn and take our journey. In the midst of challenges in this world, God expects you to move forward, grow in the Spirit and go to the next level.

As a Christian in this modern world, plunge into crisis, don't be self-satisfied and don't stay in your comfort zone. God does not expect the Christian journey to be at a standstill. Move in the power of the Holy Ghost. I see promotions, progress, and elevations from the Kingdom of God in the midst of crisis.

If the Church is to build anything of value today we must take action. In the midst of a worldwide crisis, we can progress, achieve excellence, and even receive promotions in our work, studies, marriage, home, and more.

Two

Relevance Matters

WHAT DOES IT MEAN for a church or Christian to be relevant? Primarily this is the question I guess is going on in many people who may pick up this book to read.

First, it is a fundamental question, and second, we need to get an understanding.

Cambridge dictionary defines relevance as the quality or state of being closely connected or appropriate.

To thrust deeper, how deeply connected one is to a situation of importance is the measure of relevance. As the Church of Jesus Christ, how deeply connected we are to the situation in the world today is what will determine our relevance.

The definition that caught my attention is the one that views relevance as something important to the Matter at hand. But, on the other hand, Matter is anything that has weight and can occupy space.

The world is going through a change and shift that the Church cannot ignore. But on the other hand, the Church cannot close its eyes to what is going on today. We must be closely connected to offer appropriate solutions in the midst of the global crisis.

We are at the center of it all, and I believe prophetically, believers and the Church hold the key to answering all these problems.

Therefore, relevance is to understand why something matters. As a believer, you hold the key to the problems in your neighborhood, community, city, and nation.

This principle is important because you lose value if you do not get this as the Church of Christ. Jesus puts it this way,

> "You are the salt of the earth. But what good is salt if it has lost its flavor? Can you make it salty again? It will be thrown out and trampled underfoot as worthless. **Matthew 3:15**

In this scripture, you will agree that Jesus talks about relevance and irrelevance. The Word of God is living and active, but it requires its carries to administer life and change situations.

Just like a grain of salt can lose its relevance, the Church and believers who refuse to understand the Matter can

become irrelevant, "thrown out and trampled underfoot."

It is time for believers to understand that the body of Christ is more than Sunday-to-Sunday meetings.

The relevant Church is the one that connects with its community to influence them and not be affected to become like them.

The last line is crucial **to influence the community and not vice versa.** The Church is like the way of the ship in the sea. The proper order is for the ship to be on the water, not vice versa.

The more seawater that enters the ship will, as you may know, drown it.

The ship is a symbol of the church /believer, and the sea symbolizes the world. In God's Divine order, the Church must influence the world, and not vice versa.

Therefore, it is an error for worldly standards and systems to control the Church.

The interpretation of the definition relevance needs to be precise. But, as established in my introduction, nothing must change for the Church to be relevant when it comes to the principles of the Gospel.

For instance, it is irrelevant for a church or believer to dress like the world to change the world, or mark and piece the body like the world or compromise our anointed music to sound like it.

> **The Matter at hand is how the Church can still take the Gospel of Christ to the world beyond the crisis we have all experienced.**

Without a doubt, we have all seen the devastating nature of the world's systems through this crisis. World economies and systems have broken, and the Church holds the answers as I see it.

According to World Health Organisation (**WHO**), the Matter at hand is that over two million people (at the time of writing this book) have died since this pandemic hit the earth. Of this number, my concern is, how many are going to hell?

I am not sarcastic but genuinely concerned about the relevance of the Church beyond crisis to carry out the great commission to a dying world.

This Matter is what this book is about, so please read it very carefully and let it add value to your life and Church. In the following chapters, we will discuss what I believe are the critical things every believer and Church need to understand relevant spiritually, physically, strategically, technologically, and more.

Three

Understanding the Times and Seasons

The believer is already beyond crisis.

WE ARE AT THE **heart** of prophetic manifestation, and sometimes I wonder whether the Church is aware of the implications of all that has happened since the beginning of a new decade. Yes, it would be best to understand that the year 2020 has begun the beginning of a new decade, and since that, the world has changed.

We must become like the children of Issachar who understood the times and seasons in **1 Chronicle 12:32** (Emphasis Added).

The Bible continues to say that they knew what Israel ought to do because of the understanding of these 200 men.

> **If the Church does not seek knowledge of these times and seasons, I am afraid; we may not know what to do and be left behind in relevance.**

Already, the Church, before the coronavirus pandemic, has a lot to do, especially in Europe. But, having been in ministry for almost 15 years in the UK, my candid observation is the Church is struggling.

Currently, in the UK, it is estimated that about 4% of the population only goes to Church on Sundays before the pandemic.

If you are a Christian reading this, you will agree that you do not need a Prophet to interpret the meaning of this to you.

If this is true before the pandemic, it is only wise to think beyond it. I firmly believe God wants the Church to understand the season and the times.

This crisis, like every other one, has two impacts. **First,** it can either impact you positively or, **secondly**, negatively. Understanding God's mind in the midst of all these will help us shift things in our favor and cause the Church to be more relevant than ever before.

I see the Church becoming a solution center, especially the Church in Europe, if only we could understand the times and seasons. I see the future house of God prophesied in **Isaiah 2:2** come to pass in our days if only believers and the body of Christ tap into the times and seasons.

> "Now it shall come to pass in the latter daysThat the mountain of the Lord's houseShall be established on the top of the mountains,And shall be exalted above the hills;And all nations shall flow to it.[3] Many people shall come and say,"Come, and let us go up to the mountain of the Lord,To the house of the God of Jacob;He will teach us His ways,And we shall walk in His paths."For out of Zion shall go forth the law,And the Word of the Lord from Jerusalem."

But If we do not, on the other hand, catch the mind of God, I do not see the Church dying, but I see the Church losing more relevance in community and society, especially in Europe and America.

To every believer reading this book, this is certainly not the time of watching so much television, Netflixing, too much sleeping, and eating.

"To help you, we are in a season every believer should be spending more time with the Holy Spirit to develop the mind and attitude of Christ."

"To everything, there is a season, A time for every purpose under the heaven." **Ecclesiastics 3:1.**

What a powerful scripture this is, as it reminds us that every season is a time that carries the mind and purpose of God on earth. Every man, therefore, must understand the season to fulfill God's intended purpose.

Therefore, this season carries so much potential and opportunities for the Church to thrive, especially in areas where we have not maintained relevance in the past years. However, this will be dependent on how the Church seizes this kairos moment.

It is imperative for the Church of Christ today to understand the season and time ahead of this global shift. Therefore, as you read this book, my prayer is to awaken your sensitivity to the seasons and times we find ourselves.

Four

Maintaining Spiritual Relevance

• • • • • • • • • • •

"Stop letting the world squeeze you into its mold," **J.B Phillips**

RAY **P**RITCHARD TELLS THIS story, "A little boy was sitting in Church with his mom one day. As he looked up at the beautiful stained glass window, he saw faces in the glass. Mom, who are these people in the window? He asked. Those are the saints, she answered. The little boy thought for a while and then said, they are the ones that let light in."

What a powerful story that tells us one thing, the Church, believers, and saints are the ones that shine. In other words, the believers/saints are responsible for remaining relevant to God's Kingdom agenda.

You are relevant if you add flavor or taste to the earth.

A flavorless saint or Church is good for nothing, according to Matthew 5:14-16. Remember, you must shine.

In this chapter, my sole aim is to draw your attention to spiritual strategies you (Church) should be embarking on to become relevant beyond the global crisis. I strongly suggest not taking them lightly.

1. **Prayer and the Holy Spirit.**

For the Church to be relevant beyond crisis or pandemic, there is a need for the Church to be spiritually prayerful and closer to the Holy Spirit like never before.

We cannot do anything without the Holy Spirit and prayer because spiritual power comes only through the Holy Spirit and in our engagement in worship. Any believer or Church that does not abide by these instructions risks losing relevance and fading away.

One of the apparent observations at the start of this decade and pandemic is that many churches could not survive. One of the core reasons for this is the lack of prayer and fellowship (koinonia) with the Holy Spirit.

In March 2020, when the first lockdown hit the United Kingdom, the Lord specifically instructed me to take His Church to a deeper dimension of prayer, which led us to institute

Eight (8) slot daily prayer watches. It's been two (2) years since then, and I can confirm how God has kept His Church throughout the pandemic.

What we need to understand is that prayer is an ancient landmark. **Proverbs 22:28** tells us to, Remove not the ancient landmark, thy fathers have set.

It remains the master key and the most significant investment the Church today can make for the Church tomorrow to come and benefit.

> **Prayer is a kingdom system that authorizes God's power on earth.**

The believer's strongest weapon is prayer; if only every believer could pray the price, we would see many changes on earth. But unfortunately, many believers are not motivated to pray because of doubt, sin, and other factors.

**A church not praying is playing,
and that Church can become prey
to the teeth of the enemy.**

The secret to the successful ministry of Jesus amid sharp criticism and crisis was prayer. At least the disciples confirmed this after walking with Him for a while. Then, one day, the Bible says they asked Jesus a question about the secret to His greatness, and can you guess it?

After seeing Him do miracles and wonders, one would have thought that the question would be about that. But no, they asked Him, Rabbi, teach us to pray. **Matthew 6:5-15**

**This emphasizes that for Church
to become a prophetic voice
within and beyond a global
crisis or storm, prayer and the
ministry of the Holy Spirit are
non-negotiable.**

What can God do with a weak church/believer these last days? Nothing, I believe. Like the Church in Laodicea, God hates lukewarmness.

A lukewarm church/believer is useless and weak to God, and He only wishes to vomit such out of His mouth.

The Church today must give itself more to prayer and the Spirit. Be motivated to pray because your prayers are powerful and can make a difference. The more believers engage in prayer, worship, and fasting, it increases the power of God on earth, and this is what brings about awakening and revival.

Until the Spirit is poured from on high, we can do nothing. Isaiah 32:15. It is time for the Church needs to build the Kingdom of God with prayer and the Spirit more than any other thing.

As James 1:23–24 says, the word of God is the mirror of the soul, and we look into it to determine what changes we need to make to be presentable to God. When we are changed by the gospel, we must show these changes in our daily conduct.

We were in prayer in the upper room one night when this revelation came to me from the Lord, and that is; If the Church today will tarry in prayer and the Word, the Spirit shall grant us;

- **Sudden breakthroughs**

- **Signs and wonders.**

- **Sound from Heaven.**

- **Spiritual utterances.**

- **Shiftings in the atmosphere.**

- **Standing Up's.**

- **Setting the Holy Spirit's fire on Believers.**

- **Speaking in tongues.**

- **Salvation of souls.**

2. The Church on the Hill

The hill and mountains are usually associated with prayer. Growing up, I noticed it was a common phenomenon among believers to go to the mountains frequently. However, as we grew up, we discovered that going to the hill was only associated with prayer and spiritual strength.

The mountain or hill is not a place for eating, drinking, and watching Netflix. Instead, it is a place of prayer and the impartation of the Spirit.

If the Church should overcome the global crisis and become more relevant, our position should be on the hill and mountain top.

I know I have already given you examples, but let me add another illustration to it for more clarity.

It is about Moses and how he led a generation to overcome a crisis and remain relevant. In **Exodus 17:8-13**,

[8] While the people of Israel were still at Rephidim, the warriors of Amalek attacked them. [9] Moses commanded Joshua, "Choose some men to go out and fight the army of Amalek for us.

Tomorrow, I will stand at the top of the hill, holding the staff of God in my hand."

[10] So Joshua did what Moses had commanded and fought the army of Amalek. Meanwhile, **Moses, Aaron, and Hur climbed to the top of a nearby hill**. [11] As long as Moses held up the staff in his hand, the Israelites had the advantage. But whenever he dropped his hand, the Amalekites gained the advantage.

[12] Moses' arms soon became so tired he could no longer hold them up. So Aaron and Hur found a stone for him to sit on. Then they stood on each side of Moses, holding up his hands. So his hands held steady until sunset. [13]; as a result, Joshua overwhelmed the army of Amalek in battle.

In this story, we vividly see the position every believer/church must take to win against a pandemic like our world is experiencing. Let us open it up below.

- **The Church in crisis, battle, storm, or pandemic**. The Amalek, like Coronavirus, came to fight the people. Our world and its systems are also in a pandemic because of Coronavirus/crisis. Now, since believers and the Church are on earth, we are also in battle.

- **The Church on the hill.** Moses, Aaron, and Hur were on the mountain to pray. Here says something significant, "<u>As long as Moses held up the staff in his hand, the Israelites had the advantage. But whenever he dropped his hand, the Amalekites gained the advantage</u>."

This strategy should confirm how critical prayer plays in times of crisis.

The more we raise Christ in our midst in the place of worship, the more we win.

But, unfortunately, the opposite is also very accurate.

- **The Church in battle**. Joshua and the team were fighting on the battlefield against the Amalek. This strategy represents believers in the workplace, key workers helping to fight the virus and crisis.

This is only relevant as long as the Church commits to prayer.

- **The Church in victory (relevant Church).** Success and relevance resulted as long as Moses and the people followed God's divine instructions.

Jude 1:20 encourages the Church and every believer to build ourselves up, not down, in our most holy faith, and I believe it is manifesting victories in these last days.

3. The Sword of the Spirit.

Ephesians 6:14 tells us that one of the most potent weapons of the believer is the sword of the Spirit, which is God's Word. Today, believers are overcome by the devil because; they do not know the use of the sword of the Spirit (The Word)

Can you imagine a soldier who does not know how to use a sword? That soldier is good for nothing. The believer is a soldier and an ambassador of Christ (**2 Corinthians 5:20**)

Therefore, knowing how to use God's Word as a sword in our battle against the devil is crucial.

> **Beyond the crisis in these last days, the relevant Church must know how to effectively use God's Word.**

At the start of the new year (2021), the Spirit of the Lord communicated to me these very words,

> "The level and quality of believers in the last ten(10) years have been low, thereby affecting souls won in the Kingdom."

A significant reason is that the quality of Bible Studies in the body of Christ has been low. Therefore, today and without any offense, we have emphasized more on the prophetic so that believers do not study the Word like God wants us to.

As I said, I am not downplaying the role of the prophetic ministry in our midst, but there is no prophecy without the Word. In most instances on social media and the rest, we see the cases dramatic in the Church.

Today in most churches, the focus has been on selling oils, private jets, and strange things, all in the name of prophecy.

The way to use the sword of the Spirit (Word of God) effectively, as we ought to use it, is by being filled with the Holy Spirit, for it is the Spirit who is the strength and power behind the Word.

Just like Jesus said in **John 6:63**, "The Words I speak are Spirit and truth." Church leaders today must teach more about the Word of God and the revelation of Christ.

> **It is not that many of God's people are unteachable; they are simply untaught.**

If the Church wants to be relevant, this spiritual strategy cannot be under-emphasized.

In our ministry today, we have added to our Bible study spiritual maturity growth classes, where we are beginning to take believers into a new dimension in the Word and Christ.

Jesus is the fullest, complete, and most convincing revelation of God ever given, and as such, as brother John said, He must increase, and you decrease. (**Hebrews 1:1-3, John 3:30**).

Remember, the more we lift Him, the more the Holy Spirit magnetizes our lives. Like magnetic properties, we will draw into the Kingdom and repel satanic traps and strategies in our lives, churches, and nation.

4. The Body life image of the Church/Believers

> **Studies have shown that in the average church, about 15–20 percent are active in giving and serving in the church. If only 20 percent of a person's physical body was functioning, they would be virtually a vegetable.**

Our churches are crippled by the unwillingness of so many members to use their gifts to minister to each other (Eph 4:12, 14). The key is for all of us to recognize we are "one body ... in Christ" and to live as if that were so.

Only in union with him and with each other can we gain the humility and the strength to function in unity as part of the body of Christ.

The human body, as well as the body of Christ, is composed of "one body with many members, and these members do not all have the same function."

If any of the parts of the body tries to function other than the way it was intended, the body is crippled. All of us members are meant to "form one body," the church, and to work together in unity to function as the church.

This is how spiritually we can gain momentum through the Holy Spirit.

The relevant church/Christian is a transformed one. As said in Chapter two, the church today does not need to conform to worldly patterns and standards to gain relevance.

We can only do this by being transformed by the Holy Spirit. To conform first means to pattern oneself after another person or thing.

J. B. Phillips translates this well when he said,

> **"Stop letting the world squeeze you into its mold,"**

The forces of "this age" (the time in which sin reigns, **Romans 5:21; 7:17, 20, 23**) are invading and gaining control, forcing believers and unbelievers alike to conform to its ideals—consumerism, the desire for status and success, the pleasure principle, sex, and good looks, and so on.

The only viable spiritual solution to relevance is to refuse and turn to the Spirit for the strength to rise above the pressure. The antidote for conformity to the world is to "be transformed by the renewing of your mind."

The transforming power is the Holy Spirit, who penetrates the very core of our being and reshapes us into a new creation. The Greek term (**metamorphoō**) has given us the English

metamorphosis, meaning to be "**changing step by step**" into a new being in Christ.

> **The Spirit is the change agent, enabling us to overcome temptation and live victoriously in service to God.**

Paul describes this process as "the renewing of your mind," meaning our mindset is renewed (literally "made new again and again") by the Spirit, a lifelong process in which our thinking is rescued from the influence of the world and reprogrammed to "have in mind the concerns of God" (**Mark 8:33**).

The purpose of the renewing of our mind is so that we can "test and approve what God's will is." God's will is "good, pleasing, and perfect." We should seek God's will because it will always be best for us (8:28). May you be a spiritually relevant believer.

May the Holy Spirit empower you to maintain spiritual relevance in the midst of a world in crisis. Amen

Five

Maintaining Physical Relevance

• • • • ● ● • ● ● • •

If the Word of God is to be practical, we must start practicing it.

A MAN LEFT HIS village for the town on a bicycle. Unfortunately, he had to cycle home before sunset as the road passed through a forest. Usually, before sunset, there will be lions drinking water before dusk.

He managed to cycle to town, and on his way back, he prayed, Lord, help me pass this forest before sunset. Unfortunately, as he drew close to the forest, the unfortunate happened as he had a tire puncture.

As he got off to mend his puncture in disappointment, another biker rode past him, but instead of giving him a hand, he passed by him.

When he finally mended his puncture, he knew he would be a meal to these lions. But, as he approached the forest, he was surprised to see the other biker's bicycle on the side of the forest and no lions in sight. The lions had unfortunately pounced on him and now left.

As he got home successfully, he knelt and prayed, Lord, thank you for the puncture.

Beloved, the lesson in this story is simple but powerful. Sometimes, you have to thank God for the punctures in your life. A hole, punch, or stab may be disturbing, but if you can only focus on mending it, you may see something good come out of it.

In the same way, a crisis may act just like a puncture to distract our livelihood, but if we can get on with the physical mending, it will end up like a lifesaver.

This chapter will delve into what the Church can physically do to remain relevant beyond crisis.

1.Physically, the Church must do away with complacency.

As advised in the book of **Hebrews 12:1-2**, we must do away with selfishness, self-centeredness, and indiscipline. Complacency may also include laziness, disunity, and all manner of excuses that have weakened the Church before the pandemic.

To be sincere with you, I have a passion for the Church in Europe, and having lived there for more than a decade; I have seen the spiritual state of the Church in general.

The **covid-19** pandemic, in a way, is a blessing in disguise to the Church because it came to awaken us, and if we refuse to wake up, then may we not forget that the Lord, through this book and other genuine ways, is warning us.

The attitude of the Church before the crisis has been lacking. Many, especially in Europe and America, have been busy with our agendas, forgetting God's Kingdom agenda.

> A crisis is a great revealer, and this covid-19 pandemic came to open our eyes to the truth that all things will pass away except for the Word.

For the Church to be relevant, we must do away with such negative weights to be effective.

2. Attitude

In my opinion, the most significant change we need in these last days will shock you if I tell you.

> **We do not need to worry so much about the devil but our attitude.**

We must change our attitude toward the things of God. Beyond crisis and maintaining relevance, the Church needs more of an attitudinal change.

"Your attitude determines your altitude," **John Maxwell** once said.

In order words, how high one can climb also includes one's attitude. Therefore, believers today need the right attitude.

There are two things God can increase exceedingly and abundantly, according to **Ephesians 3:20**. These are the things you speak (pray) and how you think (attitude). This further means that the Church should concentrate on praying and our philosophy in life.

While one may be a spiritual activity (prayer), your thinking and attitude are physical.

3. Time, talent, and treasure

Physically, we must offer our time, talent, and treasures to the Kingdom of God. There is one thing every believer reading this book should understand, especially the youth, and this is, you must add flavor to the earth.

In the parable of the light in **Mark 4:21-22**, Jesus tells us to let our light shine. But the question is, how do we practically allow our lights to shine? The answer rest in our talents, gifts, skills, and abilities.

I remember the Holy Spirit asking me amid the world pandemic (March 2020): Where are the young Christian people with skills, certificates, and degrees?

> **God's responsibility is to give gifts, talents, and wisdom to His people, and our responsibility is to use these gifts, talents, and skills to solve problems in the world to advance His Kingdom on earth.**

The Holy Spirit said to me these exact words; **God will not do what we can do for ourselves.** But, do you know that God is looking at us to do many things we ask Him to do?

Where are the young Christian men and women who can use their gifts, talents, and education to build apps such as Facebook, YouTube, and WhatsApp media solely for Christ?

In **Genesis 6:14-17**, we see Noah use his skills and gifts to solve problems during a world in crisis at that time. He built an ark that today is two times the football pitch size (500 feet).

In the book of Exodus 31:1-5, it reads, "Then the Lord said to Moses, [2] "See, I have chosen <u>Bezalel son of Uri</u>, the son of Hur, of the tribe of Judah, [3] and I have filled him with the Spirit of God, with wisdom, with understanding, with knowledge and with all kinds of skills—

[4] to make artistic designs for work in gold, silver and bronze, [5] to cut and set stones, to work in wood, and to engage in all kinds of crafts. [6] Moreover, I have appointed <u>Oholiab son of Ahisamak</u>, of the tribe of Dan, to help him. Also I have given ability to all the skilled workers to make everything I have commanded you:"

In this chapter, we witness two people. God gave them skills, gifts, and wisdom to solve problems. In the same way, God has given you wisdom, understanding, and knowledge to do and make something.

> **We are shifting and changing into times and seasons where people who claim to be lovers of God need to seek knowledge and use it for God on earth intellectually.**

We live at a time when you cannot underestimate the power of being skillful. So my question is, what area in your life can you increase your skill and become an expert?

> Remember **Proverbs 22:29**, which says, "Have you seen a skillful man in their work. Therefore, he will stand before Kings and not obscure men."

It is time for the Church, especially the youth and the next generation of believers, to pursue learning, reading, and drinking from good books.

4. The Church must pursue unity

The Church beyond crisis must pursue oneness and unity. Practically, believers must work together to achieve synergy. Division, fighting one another, and issues like who has the best doctrine or the biggest Church will not take us anywhere.

We must also deal with human worship within the Church, fighting over territories, materialities, and unnecessary competition. Finally, we must stop doing the devil's bidding if we want to take the world for Christ.

A church divided or disunited cannot grow.

This last century has been an unceasing example of fighting over nonessentials in the church. Going forward, the one thing we can be sure of is that Satan will continue to want us to fight over the wrong things!

The church today needs to realise this, God's presence in our lives is based not on our external activities but on their internal trust (the one in whom we believe).

At some point in ministry, our Church stopped growing. We were doing everything, but the Church was not growing.

At a point, the Holy Spirit whispered to me in a place of prayer that He was going to prune the Church. Then, in about 4-5 months, some people began to leave the Church without any apparent reason. Some were vital leaders and even worship team members.

It wasn't easy to see this happen to our ministry, but the Holy Spirit began to send new members after leaving. As a result, the current crop of leaders was of one mind and soul. Nobody was gossiping behind the scenes, and we saw growth, including students and youth. The choir, for instance, grew stronger like never before, all because of unity.

I learned one huge lesson in that period:

The Holy Spirit cannot work in a disunited church.

Unity and oneness are so crucial that Jesus talked about it in **Mark 3:23-26,**

> [23] And he called them unto him, and said unto them in parables, How can Satan cast out Satan? [24] And if <u>a kingdom be divided against itself, that Kingdom cannot stand</u>. [25] And <u>if a house be divided against itself, that house cannot stand</u>. [26] And if Satan rises up against himself, and be divided, he cannot stand, but hath an end.

A true sign of maturity of a believer or Church is its practical demonstration of maturity. Just like you will not hand over something as precious as a car key to a child to drive, God cannot trust us with kingdom greatness if we remain spiritually immature and babies.

> And I, brethren, could not speak unto you as unto spiritual, but as unto carnal, even as unto <u>babes in Christ</u>. [2] I have fed you with milk, and

not with meat: for hitherto ye were not able to bear it, neither yet now are ye able.

[3] For ye are yet carnal: for <u>whereas there is among you envying, and strife, and divisions</u>, are ye not carnal, and walk as men? [4] For while one saith, I am of Paul; and another, I am of Apollos; are ye not carnal?

[5] Who then is Paul, and who is Apollos, but ministers by whom ye believed, even as the Lord gave to every man? [6] I have planted, Apollos watered; but God gave the increase. [7] So then neither is he that planteth anything, neither he that watereth; but God that giveth the increase. **1 Corinthians 3:1-7 (KJV)**

As the early Church was of one heart and soul, so should the Church today pray and practically demonstrate our relevance and survival in some instances.

I, therefore, the prisoner []of the Lord, []beseech you to walk worthy of the calling with which you were called, **2** with all lowliness and gentleness, with longsuffering, bearing with one another in love, **3** endeavoring to <u>keep the unity of the Spirit in the bond of peace</u>. **4** There is one body and one Spirit, just as you were called in one hope of your calling; **5** one Lord, one faith, one baptism; Ephesians 4:1-6

Practically, the Church today must unite on the doctrine of Christ and His Gospel and nothing else.

The workings and sacrifices of Christ join us in the first place, and this must continue to be the basis that connects us.

He is and should remain the only message that we all preach, as Paul said in **1 Corinthians 1:23a**, but we preach Christ crucified. So again, in **2 Corinthians 4:5**, he says, "For we do not proclaim ourselves but Jesus Christ as Lord and we as servants."

Then, as if that is not enough, he reiterates in **Colossians 1:28-29**,

> "Christ is our message, we preach to awaken hearts and bring every person into the full understanding of the truth."

The Church beyond crisis must preach Christ and practice genuine love. This is possible and can be done. During our 2021 Dominion Mandate Conference, I decided to put this to practice.

With the help of the Holy Spirit, I was able to bring almost 20 Pastors and various leaders of ministries together to pray for the nations. It was one of the most beautiful and powerful truths to behold.

God's presence in our lives is based not on our external activities but on their internal trust (the one in whom we believe).

May the Lord empower you, your ministry, and your church to discover even more ways to maintain relevance in your community, city, and nation. Amen

Six

Maintaining Strategic Relevance

God is not a secret to be kept.
As a believer, you must make Him
known.

A MID A WORLD IN **turmoil,** the Church needs to understand that God's heartbeat has not changed. The heartbeat of God is still souls. God desires to see every soul saved. Hell has not been made for man but the devil.

This is why the devil is working hard so that
he will not go there alone through the Spirit of
disobedience and more.

> "The Lord isn't slow about his
> promise, as some people think. No,
> he is patient for your sake. He
> does not destroy anyone but wants
> everyone to repent." **2 Peter 3:9
> (NLT)**

> "This is good and pleases God our
> Savior, [4] who wants everyone to be
> saved and to understand the truth."
> **1 Timothy 2:3-4 (NLT)**

The scriptures above establish the heartbeat
of God for a dying world, a heart of love to
reveal His righteousness and not His wrath and
judgment.

The role of the Church today is to make
the heartbeat of the Kingdom our heartbeat.
However, today's question is, how do we
evangelize when we fight a pandemic that does

not encourage talking to each other for fear of transmitting a deadly virus?

This challenge is the burden of the Church today in a time when things are changing rapidly, right before our eyes. So my opinion is that we cannot stop evangelism; we have to be strategic about it.

We must strategically go to where the fishes (souls) are.

Jesus, in the book of **John 21:1-6**, offers us ideas to carry out the great commission. But, first, remember what we have already established: that we are at a time in history when Biblical prophecies are to come to pass.

We are about to see more saved souls than unsaved if the Church strategically positions itself to manifest God's end time agenda.

Later, Jesus appeared again to the disciples beside the Sea of Galilee.[] This is how it happened. [2] Several of the disciples were there—Simon

Peter, Thomas (nicknamed the Twin),⬚ Nathanael from Cana in Galilee, the sons of Zebedee, and two other disciples.

³ Simon Peter said, "I'm going fishing." "We'll come, too," they all said. So they went out in the boat, but they caught nothing all night. ⁴ At dawn, Jesus was standing on the beach, but the disciples couldn't see who he was.

⁵ He called out, "Fellows,⬚ have you caught any fish?" "No," they replied. ⁶ Then he said, "Throw out your net on the right-hand side of the boat, and you'll get some!" So they did, and they couldn't haul in the net because there were so many fish in it. **John 20:1-6 (NLT)**

This scripture shows a confused church that lacked focus and purpose. In addition, there was a crisis; his crucifixion had already happened on the cross, which had thrown the team in disarray though He had resurrected.

For what we are driving at, let us see a church trying to fish (win souls) but catch nothing. They caught nothing because perhaps they were looking for fish (souls) in the wrong direction and strategy.

In their frustration, Jesus appears to them and gives them a new strategy,

"Throw out your net on the right-hand side of the boat, and you'll get some!"

This is what I call **strategic mission tactics**; to go where the fishes are. Every Church today must have a strategic mission tactic. What are you willing to do to win people in your community and city for Christ?

If you do not have one, then may this book inspire you to get one. Let me offer a few suggestions beginning with the statistics before the Covid-19 pandemic.

Before the coronavirus pandemic in the UK, research concluded that only 4% of the population were churchgoers. The majority of the people spend more time online (Facebook, Youtube, Amazon) and the likes.

The question now is, **what is the right strategy for the Church to remain relevant beyond crisis if almost 80% of the people are online?** Secondly, **Where can you take the Gospel?**

If we seek, like Jesus, to use the right strategy, the Church must;

• ● ● ● ● ● ● ● ● ● •

1.Have a robust online presence moving forward.

This is one of the strategic ways your ministry can get into people's hearts and homes with the definite aim of introducing the Gospel to them.

Any church that refuses to use any of these strategies suggested in this book may survive but risk being relevant in these last days, and I have maintained that irrelevance need not be the focus in the Kingdom of God.

2.Community Engagement:

Again, strategically, the Church must be involved in the community to remain relevant.

> **The time when the Church was all about big conferences, Sunday to Sunday clapping of hands may not be over, but we must get into the community.**

For fellowship, spiritual impartation, and encouraging one another, we must continue to meet as we always do. **Hebrews 10:25** (KJV),

"Not forsaking the assembling of
ourselves together, as the manner
of some is; but exhorting one
another: and so much the more, as
ye see the day approaching."

However, the altar should not remain there.
Instead, we must raise the pulpit in the
community. What do I mean by this? I hear
someone saying?

Permit me to use our ministry, Newjoy
Int'l Gospel Church, as an example. In the
last couple of years, we have established
community-based initiatives to go into our local
communities every Christmas and Easter to
meet the basic need of people around where
our Church is based.

We have attracted many who would not have
heard the Gospel or listened to it under normal
circumstances. We reach out with food, clothes,
and daily provision and, in turn, seek the help of
the Holy Spirit to touch lives, and it is working.

We have attracted high-street shops like **ASDA**
(UK)to partner with us to reach out more. Not so
long ago, we sought and gained permission to

one of the high-rated prisons in our city, and we were granted permission to visit inmates and give gifts while sharing the Word.

All these are what I mean by taking your pulpit beyond Sunday service.

We must raise the pulpit in the community.

3.Innovation and Change

During the coronavirus pandemic, this virus forced world leaders and various governments to shut down economies, including the Church. At least from the church perspective, the only way many of us knew how to do ministry was our meeting in buildings.

So when the lockdown came, it affected many of us, if not all. Our programs and itineraries were all affected.

This meant that we all needed to find ways to do ministry. This taught me the lesson of innovation and change as a necessity in ministry. So today, without apology, I will say technology is one of the strategic points of relevance for the Church.

The principle of the Gospel must not change, but the method of administering it much change. Therefore, I agree with **Dan Reiland's** statement,

> **"Technology alone insists that you change your approach to ministry."**

May the Lord empower His church to maintain strategic relevance in our cities and nations. Amen

Seven

Standard Bearers

• • • • ● • ● ● • • •

God can do amazing things if we take
our position as standard-bearers.

LIFE IS LIVED ON levels, experienced in
stages but established in dimensions. The
relevant Church, beyond crisis, must raise the
standard. Again, I hear in my Spirit that God
is looking for standard-bearers. But, again, the
Holy Spirit said to me these exact words;

In the last decade, the quality of believers and the Church has been shallow, thereby affecting results.

From my Pastoral point of view, in the last 13 years, I will define the majority of Christians today by two standards. These standards include **Christians who live by the standard of popular opinions** and **Christians who live by emotions.** Permit me to shed more light on these.

The standard of popular opinions involves believers who live life by going with the flow. They flow with the world's standards, such as materiality and what many consider trends. But the fact that everybody is doing something does not necessarily mean that you should also do the same as a Church.

Apostle John in **1 John 2:15-16** edifies the Church,

[15] Do not love or cherish the world or the things that are in the world. If

anyone loves the world, love for the Father is not in him.

[16] For all that is in the world—the lust of the flesh [craving for sensual gratification] and the lust of the eyes [greedy longings of the mind] and the pride of life [assurance in one's own resources or in the stability of earthly things]—these do not come from the Father but are from the world [itself].

To be God's standard-bearer involves denying yourself what people are following in the world to follow His Kingdom plan.

The standard of emotions involves believers who live by their feelings. The danger is that emotions can swing both up or down, high or low. You cannot walk the Christian life controlled by your feelings, such as anger, desires, and sensuality.

I know many believers who will not pray, evangelize or even attend Church just because they do not feel like doing so. The Church beyond covid must move from this standard.

There is, however, a **third** standard by which every believer and Church must raise. This is **the standard of God's Word and the testimony of Christ**.

I have maintained the truth that a major key the Church need to be relevant is the Word of God and the testimony of Christ. If we are to embrace these two, then we are blessed. I like the saying of **Randall Mcbride Jr**, which says,

> **"Success will not lower its standard to us. We must raise our standard to success."**

The relevant Church will raise its standard to the Word of God and the revelation of Christ.

• • • • • • • • • •

Standard Bearer Defined

To raise your standard, you must first define your standard. Permit me to ask you, therefore, what is your ideal? It would help if you first answered this question because everyone has standards.

- A standard is a rule of measurement. Simply, It is how you measure yourself and, in this case, as a believer or Church. Some of us are satisfied with the title Christian on our heads, especially when we appear at an event and are introduced as Christian.

If you are such a person, then that is your standard.

- Secondly, a standard is also a level of excellence. What constitutes excellence to you?

However, the definition I believe the Holy Spirit wants to draw our attention to is from the Hebrew word '**Nec**,' which means something lifted such as a flag or banner.'

Every army is prepared for battle. Therefore, a soldier who is not battle-ready or does not know how to use a weapon is useless to his battalion and country. Besides this, the battlefield can be so chaotic that soldiers can be cut off from their units, which can be dangerous to the soldier and his mission.

To avoid this, there is a code every soldier must adhere to on the battlefield. This is in alignment with the flag or banner used in battles. The flag and banner of an army are called standard.

Therefore, it is a great honor for any soldier to have the duty to raise the flag during war or battle. The flag in combat is not for decoration but represents the pride and purpose of the army or battalion.

As long as the flag or banner is raised, it signifies faith and hope and helps soldiers stay in the ranks. The person who holds the flag (standard) is called a **standard-bearer**, and must abide by a rule or an order that he must always strive to keep.

Never let the flag touch the ground is the standing order.

Let us now turn our attention to the Church or believer. Every believer needs to fundamentally understand that you are a soldier of the Kingdom of God. **2 Corinthians 5:20** speaks very clearly on this.

> "So we are Christ's ambassadors;
> God is making his appeal through us.
> We speak for Christ when we plead,
> "Come back to God**!"**

Kindly re-read the above scripture. You are also an ambassador of the Kingdom of God as a soldier. An ambassador represents a king at the court of another kingdom. So on earth, we represent Christ to do God's kingdom business.

Christianity and life are war, a fight, and a battle, just like a soldier on the battlefield. In writing this book, the Holy Spirit revealed to me that;

The average believer does not know how to use the sword of the Spirit, which is God's Word.

And remember what I said earlier in this chapter, any believer or soldier who does not know how to use his weapons is useless to his regiment and country—May we not be futile and irrelevant believers in the body of Christ in these last days.

The relevant Church, beyond crisis, must negotiably raise the standard, flag, and banner.

Jesus Christ is the banner or flag in the Kingdom of God, and we must raise Him in our churches and lives.

A standard-bearer from God's Kingdom dimension is the believer lifting Christ and nothing else. As a kingdom soldier, ambassador, and standard-bearer, you must live by the code to never let Christ touch the ground in the standing order.

It is imperative to emphasize the role of the Holy Spirit in all of these. His role is to strengthen the Church and believers to continue to lift Christ. Only when we continue to lift Christ will He draw men and repel the devil in our communities and nations.

The role of the Holy Spirit is to magnetize our churches and lives to draw men and win souls for the Kingdom of God. This should be the position of the relevant Church in these last days. **Rev. Dr. Steve Asante** calls this serving the Lord with an Apostolic attitude.

> **The relevant Church, beyond crisis, must negotiably raise the standard, flag, and banner.**

Our brother John, the Baptiser, let us into a kingdom secret in **John 3:31** when he said, He (Christ) must increase (lifted), and I decrease. (Emphasis added). The more Christ increases and you fall, the more relevant your life and ministry become.

Therefore, the life of Christ, including His mind and attitude, must so much increase in us so that we shall begin to show good results from our salvation.

In **John 12:31-32**, Jesus, in speaking about the power of the cross, said, "The time for judging this world has come, when Satan, the ruler of this world, will be cast out. [32] And when I am lifted up from the earth, <u>I will draw everyone to myself</u>."

In the words of Christ, two exciting things are going to happen when believers lift the standard of Christ; Satan, the ruler of this world, will be cast out, and men will be drawn to Christ.

Think of it like a magnetic force when the flag of Christ is raised in the Church and the nations. As standard-bearers, the power of Christ fights the devil and draws men to Himself. Permit me to reecho the foundation and premise of this book, and that is,

God is looking for quality believers and churches.

Therefore, this chapter means men and women who will raise Christ in the Church and nothing less.

As the Church of Christ, we must not compromise on our standards. For instance, the standard of Holiness, Love, Righteousness, and the Spirit's fruit must not be compromised.

This should not only be limited to spiritual activities but also physical, emotional, and intellectual.

I love how King Solomon once put it in his book, Proverb. He said, "Remove not the ancient landmark, which thy fathers have set." **Proverbs 22:28**

This is so important because when you compromise on standards, everything declines.

When the believer's standard falls, the light of the Gospel diminishes, and darkness begins to rule.

We are the light of the world. However, when light refuses to shine, darkness will rule. In science, darkness is defined as the absence of light; cold is the absence of heat.

This means that, in theory, there is nothing like darkness or cold. On the contrary, both dark and light exist only if light and heat stop operating.

Therefore, today's relevant Church must reach the highest standards possible in everything, irrespective of the battles, storms, or crises.

Today, the relevant Church must learn to deal with uncertainties, work through tough times, and understand what it means to move from faith to faith.

• • • • ● • ● ● • • •

HOW CAN THE CHURCH BECOME CHRIST'S STANDARD BEARERS?

All that this book suggests should be considered standards the Church needs to lift in high esteem. For the sake of this chapter, I will deepen with ink three (3) of the essential standards.

1. **Scripture**: If you are to raise your standard as a saint, the Word must be lifted. Jesus is the living Word, and the Bible is the written Word. The Living Word is revealed in the written Word, and the written Word leads us to the Living Word.

Jesus' parable of the Sower is an excellent example to the Church today. (**Matthew 13:1-9, 18-23**.)

2. **Spirit**: Scripture (the Word) cannot work without the Spirit because the Holy Spirit is the power of the Word. To live a life without the Spirit will only make you a canal believer. Therefore, there is a need for the Church to balance spirituality with physicality to maintain relevance.

Jesus's parable of the ten virgins is a good source of example.

3. **Sacrifice and commitment**: Raising or lifting the standard we do things in the Church or in our lives requires sacrifice and dedication. God is looking for quality believers who will give their all to Him.

We can talk of Scripture and Spirit, but the real question is,

Are you willing to sacrifice your desires, goals, and priorities to raise Christ as your standard?

And so, dear brothers and sisters,[ ]
I plead with you to give your bodies
to God because of all he has done
for you. Let them be a living and
holy <u>sacrifice</u>—the kind he will find
acceptable. This is truly the way to
worship him. **Romans 12:1 (NLT)**

Prayer: May the Lord empower you to become
His end-time standard bearer in this world.

Eight

Leadership Change

● • ● • ● • ● • ● • ● • ● • ●

"Everything rises and falls on leadership." **John Maxwell**

WHILE WRITING THIS BOOK, I had an opportunity to visit a church in **Barnsley**. It was Christmas, and we were still in the pandemic. Our Church decided to reach out to people in the community especially struggling individuals and families, with the love of Christ through what we call the "Christmas Community Giveaway."

At the height of the pandemic, we reached out to **Armley Prisons (Leeds**) with over 180 pay of warm items for the winter. In addition, we supported over **80 families** with food items and gifts, plus helping many in our communities.

During this time, we heard of **Pastor Mick** in the city of Barnsley. His ministry is called Church on the Street. This man served his community to the level that the British Broadcasting Corporation (**BBC)** ran a documentary on him.

Through this documentary, the Lord reached out to us to contact him.

He accepted our invitation, and together with other leaders and members of the Church, we drove for about an hour and a half to the city of Barnsley to bless his ministry and also contribute food items to his food bank.

Little did I know that God was taking me to this ministry to show me a picture of a relevant church. Everything the Lord has revealed to me in this book is already implemented in this ministry.

We discovered, for instance, that they have their regular Sunday service in the morning but inside the Church is a section designated for anyone to have a free haircut and another for women to have their pedicure and manicure.

Every Monday to Friday, Pastor Mick and his team are open from 8:30 am-3 pm for drop-ins, where the Church is available to the community to get hot food and drinks.

In addition, they have succeeded in working with the local authority to help people with housing, benefits, and other needs.

They have days for mental health and addiction support and recovery groups within the week. We met men and women who were formal Muslims, drug addicts, and prostitutes but have now given their lives to Christ through this ministry.

They are the people who now form the evangelism team of the Church.

This proves that every divine idea suggested in this book is applicable. But first, we, the Church of Christ, can do it amid a crisis or beyond. Secondly, it will take leaders' change in thinking and attitude to make this happen, and this is where the focus of this chapter is.

• • ● ● ● • ● ● ● ● •

Leadership

Leadership is one of the biggest challenges of the Church becoming relevant or influential beyond crisis. The relevant Church needs relevant leaders.

> **We need leaders who will understand and, most importantly, implement the mind of God.**

As you have witnessed throughout this book, things have shifted and changed, and leaders need to move and adjust to maintain relevance beyond the crisis. But, again, it is about being deliberate in your leadership.

We cannot implement the solutions offered in this book without a leadership change. Every leader needs to change to maintain relevance beyond the crisis. I know by now that you are convinced the difference is not related to the principles of the Gospel but its functions.

Paul writes to his protégé Timothy amid crisis and charges him,

> "But you, Timothy, certainly know what I teach, and how I live, and what my purpose in life is. You know my faith, my patience, my love, and my endurance. [11] You know how much persecution and suffering I have endured." **2 Timothy 3:10-11a.**

The seven (7) things underlined in the verse above are crucial to every leader today to maintain relevance at such a time.

1. **What I Teach**: You certainly know how I

teach.

Let's start with this question, **what do you teach as a leader in the Church?** This is vital because what you teach will determine your relevance in your community and beyond.

We need Pastors and leaders in our denominations to teach the accurate Word of God in these changing times. One of the things we lack in the body of Christ today is spiritually mature believers.

> **Canality is a deceptive weapon of the devil, and as long as the Church remains in the flesh, it will be seemingly impossible to stay relevant.**

Therefore, the answer to a guaranteed relevant Church or believer is living by the Spirit's power. I believe that the responsibility of every church leader goes beyond winning souls. Every church leader amid this crisis and beyond owe it to God to raise Spiritually matured believers.

> "This will continue until we all come to such <u>unity in our faith</u> and <u>knowledge of God's Son</u> that we will be <u>mature in the Lord</u>, measuring up to the <u>full and complete standard of Christ</u>." **Ephesians 4:13 (NLT).**

The scripture above fits the kind of leaders God requires these last days. Leaders who will lead through crisis to build believers growing in their faith and knowledge of Christ. Leaders who will raise mature Christians who fit the standard of the Holy Spirit.

The secret is this;

Victory is not secured in these crisis times until the Spirit takes over.

As leaders teach and raise firm, mature believers, there is hope for a dying world.

This is when your fruits have abode. Jesus put it this way,

You have not chosen Me, but I have chosen you, and I have appointed and placed and purposefully planted you, so that you would go and bear fruit and keep on bearing, and that your fruit will remain and be lasting.
John 15:16 (AMP)

2. How I Live: You certainly know how I live.

> **We need leaders
> who practice
> what they
> preach.**

For many years, this has become a fundamental principle in my life. There is no point in having leaders who say one thing and do otherwise. Instead, we need leaders today who live in the knowledge of the truth they preach.

Ralph Waldo Emerson was right when he said,

> **"**Who you are speaks so loudly I can't hear what you are saying.**"**

We need Christian leaders with integrity, character, self-control, and discipline today more than ever before.

The relevant Church requires such leaders to lead the next generation at this time. Therefore, the phrase "how you live" or "practice what you preach" is not just an idea but a principle that should never be overlooked.

It is grounded in Jesus' rebuke of the hypocritical Pharisees in His days.

> "For they preach, but do not practice." **Matthew 23:3 (ESV).**

If church leaders preach good words but fail to practice what they preach, then our preaching will not demonstrate any power, affecting the people.

Preaching Bolt and Nuts is one of my favorite books. In it, author **Brandon Hilgemann** says,

"Good preaching is persuasive preaching. If not, it is fluffy words with no power. A gospel preaching is more than words. It is the sum of a preacher's character, passion, and words."

If your words will be full of power, then how you live matters. Therefore, the relevant Church requires leaders to live in the living Word of God.

3. My Purpose in Life: You certainly know my purpose in life.

Again, we need leaders who know and understand their purpose in life. Leaders who have a purpose will help pull people up in the midst of this worldwide crisis. The relevant Church in these last days requires such leaders.

"The two most important days in your life are the days you were born and the day you discover why you were born." **Mark Twain.**

Again this is why we need leaders who will help people discover the why of their lives, especially in a crisis. The current global pandemic is enough to push people into fear and discomfort.

Millions of people have already given up on the Church, youth groups, or organizations. So if you are a leader at home, family, institution, or Church, God wants you to first focus on purpose and help the people around you to find their reason for being in the midst of the crisis.

It is a worldwide truth that people with purpose live better than people without. **Naina Dhingra, Jonathan Emmett, Andrew Samo, and Bill Schaninge**, in their article Igniting individual purpose during a crisis, said

> "During times of crisis, individual purpose can be a guidepost that helps people face up to uncertainties and navigate them better, and thus mitigate the damaging effects of long-term stress. Igniting individual purpose in times of crisis.

The Rush Memory and Aging Project, which began in 1997, finds that when comparing patients who say they have a sense of purpose with those who say they don't, the former is:

- 2.5 times more likely to be free of dementia

- 22 percent less likely to exhibit risk factors for stroke

- 52 percent less likely to have experienced a stroke

All these are evidence that proves that we need leaders who are purposefully strong to lead and help others live on purpose lives at such a time like we are seeing all over the world.

4. **My Faith**: You certainly know my faith.

Another critical leadership quality needed to maintain relevance is faith. To every leader, faith is as essential spiritually as money is physical. The Kingdom of God functions by faith, and without it, it is impossible to please God.

We need faith-full leaders, especially in times of crisis. This is because the central task of a leader is to imagine a better future beyond challenges and inspire their followers to get there.

Therefore, a great leader is a risk taker because there may be no guarantees to outlast crisis, but they continue in optimism because of faith. This is what pleases God.

People look up to their leaders during times of crisis, so a leader's growth of faith can directly impact those they lead.

For example, at the height of Isreal in crisis, God told Joshua immediately after the death of Moses to be bold and courageous. Then, in Joshua 1:6-9, He said it over five times to the young leader Joshua.

As leaders leading in such difficult times, we should not lose our bold, courageous faith simply because of our survival and the survival of those we lead. Someone said,

"Faith helps leaders remain aware of their vulnerabilities without eroding their confidence, and it sustains them when they must pursue values and visions that put them and their organizations at risk."

I love **Hebrews 11**, a chapter I fondly call the 'hall of faith' as against the 'hall of fame in Hollywood. This chapter reminds every leader to learn to lead through tough times with faith and confidence.

The patriarchs in this beautiful chapter remind us that we are surrounded by such a great cloud of a witness who stood firm throughout crisis and challenges to win, and we, in turn, can do the same, especially as we have Christ to look up to.

5.   **Patience**: You certainly know my patience.

Patience is a virtue. One that is easy to talk about but difficult to practice, especially in leadership. It is one of the fundamental principles that have decided many leaders' success. On the other hand, impatience has also decided many leaders' failures.

Webster defines patience as "the quality of being capable of bearing affliction calmly." In his article, Leading with Patience – the Will to Wait, **Doug Moran** said,

> "True leaders recognize that patience enables them to take stock of the situation, understand what is required, and wait while building the capacity to take appropriate, effective action. By demonstrating patience, leaders reinforce the importance of focusing on long-term outcomes.

This is how God wants every leader to lead. Tough times don't last, but tough leaders do.

A true, relevant leader can point people to a long-term vision and help them get there irrespective of difficulties.

Patience does not mean stopping and doing nothing or being inactive. It instead means to continue to serve your way out to greatness. So Paul writes to Timothy to encourage him to continue in service in the same way he had patiently endured through tough times in ministry.

So to every leader reading this chapter, know that it begins with you. Patience builds your character and attitude to lead.

> "A positive attitude is something everyone can work on, and everyone can learn how to employ it." **Joan Lunden**.

It is what prepares you to become productive and effective. You can get the best out of every crisis if you first take the time to prepare and wait. **Abraham Lincoln** said,

> "If I had six hours to chop down a tree, I would spend the first four hours sharpening the axe."

6.   **Love**: You certainly know, my love.

At the heart of genuine leadership is love. Leaders will be relevant in the Church today if they lead in love, especially during a crisis period. This is what Paul was teaching Timothy to emulate under his ministry.

The relevant Church, in this sense, is one where the people, be it local believers or the community at large, can feel that someone genuinely cares about their needs and welfare. The feeling that people at the helm of affairs have our genuine interests at heart.

> **Leadership has a powerful impact on people when the people feel loved.**

My visit to Pastor Mick's Church showed me the power of love and its relationship to a relevant church. We met people who had been moved out of the street to Christ by the leadership of this Church.

> Love is the sacred quality THAT enables individuals to willingly give themselves to help others to achieve their highest potential and to create a better world**.**

Stephen R. Covey, the American author, scholar, and motivational speaker is also recognized for his emphasis on the importance of love and his wisdom in applying true principles associated with human behavior.

> Covey believed that love, trust, and treating people with a commitment to helping them achieve their greatest possible potential were fundamental responsibilities of leaders.

This is why **1 Corinthians 13** (chapter of love) is so vital for every leader these last days. No Matter what you do as a leader, it is nothing if love is not at its center.

It begins with loving yourself first as a leader and fully recognizing the goodness you possess to love the Church of Christ, primarily through a crisis. This reminds me of Jesus and Simon Peter at the time. Jesus knew the situation the Church would face after leaving earth.

> When they had finished breakfast, Jesus said to Simon Peter, 'Simon, son of John, <u>do you love me more than these?</u>' Peter said to him, 'Yes, Lord; you know that I love you.' Jesus said to him, 'Feed my lambs'

> "16He said to him a second time, 'Simon, son of John, <u>do you love me</u>?' Peter said to him, 'Yes, Lord; you know that I love you.' He said to him, 'Tend my sheep'

> "17Jesus said to Peter the third time, 'Simon, son of John, <u>do you love me</u>?' Peter was grieved because he said to him the third time, '<u>Do you love me</u>?' and he said to him, 'Lord, you know

everything; you know that I love you.' Jesus said to him, 'Feed my sheep'" **(John 21:17, ESV)**.

The proof of authentic leadership is love. In the conversation above, Jesus tested Peter on love. He knew there was a crisis ahead, and the only way Peter could lead and maintain relevance was centered on his passion for Him.

> **The leader's love for himself and the people he leads is key to their manifestation of victory over challenges and difficult times.**

7.   Endurance: We are living in times where it will take strength and endurance to maintain relevance in the body of Christ. Any believer or Church that quickly gives up stands the risk of being overcome by the current crisis.

This is why every leader needs to lead with endurance. Leadership endurance is the ability for one to remain steadfast and unmoveable in a time of uncertainty.

Paul wrote Timothy to encourage Timothy to endure a crisis. We need leaders today who can lead through hard times. Leaders will empower people to keep going irrespective of the obstacles and pressures.

One of my favorite chapters in the Bible is Hebrews 11, which I fondly call "the hall of faith." I am reminded of different dispensational leaders who run their race with endurance without giving up whenever I read this chapter.

As I have repeatedly said throughout this book, we are not the only generation that has faced a crisis.

However, crisis is part of the human race, and since we have examples of men and women who have led successfully through endurance, we also need to learn to lead the Church of Christ and our lives with endurance.

So in Hebrews 12:1, after calling out leaders who led with endurance, the writer charges every believer, especially leaders, with these very words.

Therefore, since we are surrounded by such a great cloud of witnesses, let us throw off everything that hinders and the sin that so easily entangles. And let us run with perseverance the race marked out for us, [2] fixing our eyes on Jesus, the pioneer and perfecter of faith. For the joy set before him he endured the cross, scorning its shame, and sat down at the right hand of the throne of God. [3] Consider him who endured such opposition from sinners, so that you will not grow weary and lose heart.

First, We are surrounded by a great cloud of witnesses. In order words, we have all around us leaders who kept moving forward in the midst of pain and uncertainty. Leaders like Abraham, Isaac, Noah, Samson, and others witness the truth that tough times may come, but tough leaders outlast crises.

Secondly, let us fix our eyes on Jesus. It is refreshing that around us are people who hold success stories of endurance, and at the very top sit Christ, the author and finisher of our faith.

We have the Patriarch as our examples and Jesus as our focus, and because of these, you cannot fail in your leadership

One major secret to Jesus's successful ministry on earth is endurance and perseverance. He did this by seeing the joy set before Him. When the leader can see beyond challenges and uncertainties, it helps them remain relevant longer than the crisis.

When I lift my eyes, I see the relevant Church. I positively see the Church of Christ situated in the mountains and many people are going there for protection, deliverance, and salvation. Oh, what a joy and time for the Church of Christ to shine, arise and flourish like the palm tree.

Prayer: May your life, ministry, and Church be even more relevant in these uncertain and last days. Shalom, peace, and Newjoy to you.

Nine

A Revival Generation

• • • ● ● ● • ● ● ● • •

"The book of acts was written because the apostles acted." **Smith Wigglesworth**

THE RELEVANT **C**HURCH IS **also** preparing a new generation of men and women God is raising for His end-time agenda. In the middle of writing this book, God showed me that a miraculous revival is imminent and it will require a new generation to prokove it.

If the Church of Christ is going to be relevant in these last days, then this must be at the top of our agenda.

In a vision, the Lord showed me ten (10) characteristics of this new generation. In this chapter, I will share these ten characteristics to empower Church leaders and elders to prepare.

1. **God is raising a new generation that will begin to see problems as opportunities.** At the heart of a world in crisis, the Church can either join the world to see problems, talk about problems or do something about the crisis.

   For the Earth will be filled with the knowledge of the glory of the Lord as the waters cover the sea."
   – Habakkuk 2:14 (KJV)

The Church will become and maintain relevance if we see and take this great opportunity to provoke a miraculous revival in the nations of the world.

A new generation needs to arise to see things from heaven's perceptive and not the earth.

> Arise, shine; for thy light is come, and the glory of the LORD is risen upon thee. For, behold, the darkness shall cover the earth, and gross darkness the people: but the LORD shall arise upon thee, and his glory shall be seen upon thee. And the Gentiles shall come to thy light, and kings to the brightness of thy rising. **Isaiah 60:1-3 (KJV)**

2. God is raising a new revival generation that will be highly characterized by prayer, fasting, and holiness and carries the pure and naked fire of the Holy Spirit.

The chapter on maintaining spiritual relevance throws more light on this but permit me to share a bit more.

Prayer is a man getting connected to God because he realizes that everything that works is connected to a power source. We need power, and the only way the relevant church gets power is to be connected to the Holy Spirit's power.

> **Smith Wigglesworth** was right when he said, "The book of acts was written because the apostles acted."

The relevant Christian recognizes the need to act in accordance with the Holy Spirit as the apostles did in their time.

Secondly, prayer is a man calling on God to help solve problems on earth. Just like the early Church maintained relevance through prayer, so this new generation needs to rise up in prayer if we are to provoke a revival.

> If my people, who are called by my name, will humble themselves and pray and seek my face and turn from their wicked ways, then I will hear from heaven, and I will forgive their sin and will heal their land. **2 Chronicles 7:14 (KJV)**

There are two groups of people I see at the heart of God's end-time agenda in the Church. You must either have caught a level of the fire of the Holy Spirit or be willing and ready to receive this fire.

Those with a cool-down attitude or watered-down Christianity are not part of this revival generation, I see.

> Relevance is not possible without the fire of the Holy Spirit.

3. God is raising a new revival generation with a strong purpose and vision. The relevant Church must have a clear purpose and vision that sees beyond the world in crisis.

The mystery of life is finding yourself and losing yourself.

For the church to become relevant in the world, God is raising a new generation that will first find themselves and impact the nations with what they discover.

- The relevant believer is not about self but about others.

- The relevant believer is not about getting power but seeking to empower others.

- The relevant believer will not focus on the how but the why.

In **Luke 10**, Jesus called the disciples and sent them two by two to go preach the gospel. As part of His instructions to them, He commissioned them not to take any money.

At a time when the world is in crisis, many people are asking where we in the church are going to get the finances to overseeing many of the suggestions offered in this book.

The answer lies in Luke 22:35 (NASB);

> "And He said to them, "When I sent you out without money belt and bag and sandals, you did not lack anything, did you?" They said, "No, nothing."

The assurance here is God's work done in God's way will never lack God's provision. People do not just give to people but to vision and purpose. Money is never a problem to God as long as we do what He has instructed us to do.

4. God is raising a new revival generation that He is going to provide for them.

Again, the issue of Kingdom finances in the midst of crisis should not be a problem. When Abraham had to obey God in a time of difficulty, God provided for Him and I see God raising a new generation to make His Kingdom relevant in the heart of local communities and societies with that same strategy.

> And Isaac said to his father Abraham, "My father!" And he said, "Here I am, my son." He said, "Behold, the fire and the wood, but where is the lamb for a burnt offering?" Abraham said, "God will provide for himself the lamb for a burnt offering, my son." So they went both of them together.
> **Genesis 22:7-8 (ESV)**

I have shared in the chapters of this book how God instructed us to start feeding the needy and poor in our city. So we started what we call "Free Hot Drink and Meal". As at February 2023, we have served over 2000 meals for free and never lacked supply or provision in the midst of a global crisis. The relevant church has God as their Jireh.

> May you never underestimate God's ability to do what He says He will do.

5. God is raising a revival generation that will be alert, aware, awake and active. This church of Christ will not allow the current economic crisis to intimidate them.

> [8] Be <u>alert</u> and of sober mind. Your enemy the devil prowls around like a roaring lion looking for someone to devour. **1 Peter 5:8 (NIV)**

> The thief comes only to steal and kill and destroy; I have come that they

may have life, and have it to the full.
John 10:10 (NIV)

Both of these scriptures encourage this new generation to be alert, awake, and active. If you are reading this book and you feel a staring and burden in your heart, then you are showing signs of those God is raising for the nations. Understand timing and be weary of those I call "**firefighters**."

These are people close to or around you who can quench the fire of the Holy Spirit in you. On the contrary, be on the lookout for "**fireLighters**." These, on the other hand, are people close to or around you that will fan the flame of the Holy Spirit unto relevance.

For starters, I hope this book lights up your fire.

6. God is raising a new revival generation that will be very discerning. Discernment is one of the key requirements for this end-time. The relevant church is one which is able to discern the time and season so as to avoid

Satan's greatest weapons in the midst of a world in crisis. These are distraction and deception.

7. God is raising a new revival generation that will recognise a need and cooperate fully for the greater good. One is too small a number to achieve significance. It is an African proverb that says,

> **"If you want to go fast, go alone, but if you want to go far, go with people."**

8. God recognizes that people are the greatest resources needed to achieve His purpose. He is, therefore, strategically raising the right people, teams, and groups. The fulfillment of every great vision includes people. I see youth groups forming in churches and Universities to this effect.

At the heart of everything shared in this book, I do not only see God raising Pastors and Church workers. Some of these groups will include Medical Doctors, Engineers, Multi-Millionaires, and more for Kingdom relevance on earth in these last days.

In the midst of these prophecies, our ministry has launched a **Student Christian Union** at the premier University in our City.

What we see is God pouring out His fire upon young men and women to prepare them to impact the nations for a miraculous revival and relevance.

9. God is raising a new revival generation that will rise and build with speed. The book of Nehemiah is one inspirational writing I highly will recommend you to read due to the crisis he faced in rebuilding the wall of his city.

At a time when men thought it was not possible to rebuild in the midst of crisis, he trusted in God's grace and did it.

In **Nehemiah 2:20**, he told his enemies,"I replied, "The God of heaven will help us succeed. We, his servants, will start rebuilding this wall. But you have no share, legal right, or historic claim in Jerusalem." And in 52 days, Nehemiah outlasted the crisis to rebuild the broken walls. Nehemiah 6:15-16.

> I see God's grace and
> power coming on this revival
> generation for relevance.

10. God is raising a new revival generation that will be balanced. God has said in the book of **Proverbs 11:1** that "A false balance is an abomination to the LORD, but a just weight is his delight."

The relevant Church is also a balanced Church. This is why this book has not only looked at one dimension of becoming relevant but beyond.

For instance, you will discover spiritual, physical, strategic, and multiple areas the Church and believers need to focus on in order to fulfill the mind of God in these last days.

> The fulfillment of every great
> vision requires hard work, passion,
> enthusiasm, and zeal on one side
> and, on the other hand, prayer
> and a close relationship with God
> and His Holy Spirit. This is the

balance generation God is raising for endtime relevance on earth.

In conclusion, it is my prayer that every Divine suggestion and solution shared in this book will inspire the Church of Jesus Christ in these crisis and last days to rise and go beyond to achieve relevance.

About Author

Kofi Amoateng Owusu is a Life Coach, Entrepreneur, Author, and Pastor. His vision is to challenge Individuals, Leaders, and Corporate Organisations to discover purpose and fulfill Significance in life.

Kofi believes that the best of human exposure and experience serves as the best form of every human communication; thus, through your pains and disappointments, one discovers his God-ordained Purpose

It was no wonder that it was from the painful experience of losing both parents earlier in his childhood and the many challenges that followed, which pushed him to discover his purpose and now fulfilling destiny.

Trained in Psychology and Sociology, Kofi possesses a Bachelor's Degree, a Certificate in Leadership and Management, and Information Technology in Ghana, the United Kingdom, and the United States of America. He has also been trained and mentored by great leadership giants like John Maxwell and the late Myles Munroe.

Over the last ten years, Kofi has mentored and fulfilled Leadership roles across nations. He currently serves as a lead consultant for the AFAP Coaching School, runs an African Restaurant (Yam Spice African Foods, UK), facilitates a weekly free Hot Drink /Meal in the City of Bradford, and is a Lead Pastor at Newjoy Int'l Gospel Church.

Kofi is a recipient of numerous Achievement and Excellence Awards in the UK and beyond. He is the author of several books, such as the best-selling Alive for A Purpose, Four Quadrants to Greatness, and more.

Kofi is married to his beautiful wife, Rhoda, and has three wonderful children.

Also By The Author

KOFI AMOATENG OWUSU
www.purposeachievinglife.com

My purpose is to love my wife, raise great children, point many to Christ, and influence many to discover purpose and raise a new generation of Leaders for global impact

BIBLIOGRAPHY

Doug Moran. Leading with Patience – The Will to Wait. https://ifyouwilllead.com/leading-with-patience-the-will-to-

Covey, S. R. (1992). Principle-Centered Leadership. New York: Simon & Schuster.

Osborne, Grant R.. Romans Verse by Verse (Osborne New Testament Commentaries) (p. 343). Lexham Press. Kindle Edition.

Hilgemann, Brandon. Preaching Nuts & Bolts: Conquer Sermon Prep, Save Time, and Write Better Messages. Brandon Hilgemann. Kindle Edition.